Stars

Based on the TV series *Peppa Pig*.
Peppa Pig is created by Neville Astley and Mark Baker

Level 1 is ideal for children who have received some initial reading instruction. Stories are told, or subjects are presented, very simply, using a small number of frequently repeated words.

Special features:

Opening pages introduce key story words

Careful match between text and pictures

Peppa wants to see the stars.

"We can go out and look," says Daddy Pig.

Large, clear type

Educational Consultant: Geraldine Taylor
Book Banding Consultant: Kate Ruttle

LADYBIRD BOOKS

UK | USA | Canada | Ireland | Australia
India | New Zealand | South Africa

Ladybird Books is part of the Penguin Random House group of companies
whose addresses can be found at global.penguinrandomhouse.com.

www.penguin.co.uk www.puffin.co.uk www.ladybird.co.uk

Text adapted from Peppa Pig: Stars, first published by Ladybird Books, 2009
This edition published 2019
007

© 2019 ABD Ltd/Ent. One UK Ltd/Hasbro
Written by Ellen Philpott

PEPPA PIG and all related trademarks and characters TM & © 2003 Astley Baker Davies Ltd and/or Entertainment One UK Ltd.
Peppa Pig created by Mark Baker and Neville Astley. HASBRO and all related logos and trademarks TM and © 2019 Hasbro.
All rights reserved. Used with Permission.

Licensed by

Printed in China

The authorized representative in the EEA is Penguin Random House Ireland,
Morrison Chambers, 32 Nassau Street, Dublin D02 YH68

A CIP catalogue record for this book is available from the British Library

ISBN: 978-0-241-36150-4

All correspondence to
Ladybird Books
Penguin Random House Children's
One Embassy Gardens,
8 Viaduct Gardens,
London SW11 7BW

MIX
Paper | Supporting
responsible forestry
FSC® C018179

It is Peppa and George's bedtime.

"George, take that space helmet off," says Daddy Pig.

George loves space.

George wants his milk.
His helmet is in the way!

Peppa helps George take
it off. George has his milk.

Peppa and George go to bed.

"What do you like about space, George?" says Peppa.

"George loves the stars,"
says Daddy Pig.

Peppa wants to see the stars.

"We can go out and look," says Daddy Pig.

"Look!" says Daddy Pig.
"That is the North Star."

Everyone wants a telescope.

"Grandpa Pig has a telescope," says Mummy Pig.

It is Grandpa Pig's bedtime.

Peppa says, "Can we see the telescope?"

"Yes, yes – this way!"
says Grandpa Pig.

"Look! This is the telescope," says Grandpa Pig. "We can see the stars."

Everyone loves the telescope.

Grandpa Pig helps Peppa to look into the telescope.

Peppa looks about. She can see the North Star.

Grandpa Pig helps George to look into the telescope.

"What can you see, George?" says Peppa.

George can see a planet.

"What planet is that?" says Peppa.

"It is Saturn," says Grandpa Pig.

George wants to go to Saturn one day.

Peppa likes the stars and planets.